MW00694962

Thriving in the Workplace with Autoimmune Disease

Know Your Rights
Resolve Conflict
Reduce Stress

HOLLY J. BERTONE, CNHP, PMP

Having an autoimmune condition or any other kind of invisible illness can be isolating. You may look and act totally fine on the outside, but you feel like your insides are slowly killing you and all you ever want to do is crawl under the covers and go to sleep.

It's difficult enough for your family and spouse to understand what you are going through. It's especially difficult in the workplace when your employer can't "see" your condition and doesn't understand why you are asking for flexibility or accommodations. You feel like no one understands. You feel like you have no voice.

The #1 Amazon bestseller, *Thriving in the Workplace with Autoimmune Disease* is the first book ever to educate individuals specifically with autoimmune disease on their legal and disability rights in the workplace. The book was born out of author Holly Bertone's personal and painful experience and lack of resources available specifically for individuals with autoimmune diseases. She walks you through the basics of navigating FMLA, EEO, reasonable accommodations, working with your boss, and then provides much needed resources to help you find that critical balance between taking care of your health and managing your symptoms at work.

This book is not going to tell you to give up and become a victim. The mission of this book is to empower you with knowledge so that you can rise above your illness and challenges and thrive both at home and in the workplace.

THANK YOU for your purchase! As a small gesture of our extreme gratitude, please accept your free eBook (and other goodies!) to launch you into the life of good health and fortitude!
Download your FREE book here:
https://pinkfortitude.com/thank/

FORWARD BY PEARL THOMAS

According to the American Autoimmune Related Disease Association (AARDA), 54 million Americans suffer from autoimmune (AI) disease and an estimated 24 million of those people suffer from Hashimoto's Thyroiditis. Hashimoto's is one of the most common yet uncommonly diagnosed diseases in the world. This disease often manifests quietly, with symptoms that are hard to see on the outside, making the diagnosis less likely, and social support sometimes hard to come by.

In *Thriving in the Workplace with Autoimmune Disease*, Holly Bertone reveals her heart-wrenching story of intense AI symptoms that affected her heavy work load. Subsequently, she was not granted the time off by her company to support the healing she needed, but instead, they used it against her. Holly's energy and attitude are infectious, and her story is poignant about struggling with AI in the workplace. By reading this book, you will learn how to become an advocate for your AI, especially when it involves your rights in the workplace. Holly provides a complete picture of the realities of managing work and AI symptoms simultaneously.

I've known Holly since 2015 when she stepped up to become an advocate for the Hashimoto's and AI community. She is a woman of heart, honor, and strength and strives to inspire change in the world. This book is a must-read for anyone with an autoimmune condition who is working a full time job.

Pearl Thomas
Founder, HeyHashi

PRAISES

"Your book is such a great resource and simple tool for those with AI to dig into without having to figure it all out themselves. Your positive attitude and caring nature are encouraging and you lead by example. Thank you Holly, for providing a tool that has been missing for those that have an invisible illness. I maintained an active and vibrant life, so when I was depleted of energy and in pain, others couldn't grasp it. It goes without saying that most people don't fully understand something unless they've actually gone through it themselves."

Christina Grenga, Grenga Health

"Based on her own personal experience, Holly has put together this guide to help others who can learn from her research. While each situation is always different and each person should look at their own legal options, this guide gives quick access and helpful information about your legal rights to save you time and energy. Holly brings forth her courage and heart to share her own experience and empower others in a way that's easy to understand so they can get legally clear and make the best decisions for them."

Lisa Fraley, JD, Legal Coach & Attorney

"Holly's in depth research and knowledge on the topic provides readers with insightful and thorough information when dealing with AI in the workplace. Additionally, she breaks down information into usable and understandable steps, and includes sample verbiage that is essential when moving through the process of applying for work accommodations. This is a must have for anyone struggling with autoimmune diseases."

McCall McPherson, Modern Thyroid Clinic

"As one of Holly's doctors, I can attest to her journey and struggle. She wanted nothing more than to figure out a way to regain her health, do well in her job, and take care of her family. This book comes from a dark time in her life, but is a much needed resource for those who have autoimmune conditions and need to balance their health and career."

Dr. Heather Paulson, ND, FABNO, The Paulson Center

A NOTE OF INTRODUCTION FROM THE AUTHOR

According to the American Autoimmune Related Disease Association (AARDA), autoimmune (AI) diseases occur in 75% of women compared to men, and predominantly during childbearing years. If your AI disease has become too tough to deal with and your financial situation is in order, you may be fortunate enough to leave the workplace altogether, or to find a less stressful part time job. But for many individuals, quitting your job is not financially prudent or possible.

For many women, in addition to working a full time job, we also have responsibilities outside of work such as taking care of our home, our spouse, our children, and even our parents. There are not enough hours in the day to accomplish everything we have to do, and being sick on top of everything makes it near impossible. Stress is a huge factor in all AI diseases that we need to keep at a minimum level. When all of these responsibilities are stacked on top of each other, our career/job is the one place we look to for flexibility and understanding.

I recently had to navigate the EEO process at my job in the federal government. My first action was to research the process online and learn what my rights are and how others have fared. My second action was to reach out to my Facebook groups and ask for help and guidance. I came up completely empty handed.

Now what? Do I file for a reasonable accommodation? Do I even qualify as having a disability? What forms do I use? How should my doctor complete the forms? Am I being discriminated against? What is legal? Who can I talk to? Why does it seem like no one understands or cares?

If this is you, please know that you are not alone. I've pulled together the research and interviewed several experts to help you navigate this complicated process. In my darkest hour, I knew in my heart that I wanted to write this book for YOU. To let you know that you are not alone.

I love feedback, so please leave a review on Amazon, or drop me a note.

You can reach me at holly@pinkfortitude.com or hit me up on social media @PinkFortitude

Thank you for letting me be a part of your quest for a healthier you.

Holly Bertone, CHNP, PMP

DEDICATION

To Stephen Beck, Jr.
June 2, 1970 – December 8, 2014

Who selflessly fought for many years to give a voice to those who are differently abled. It is because of his leadership that the Stephen Beck Jr. Achieving a Better Life Experience (ABLE) Act was passed into law, and only days after his untimely passing.

Stevie, from childhood on, you have always looked out for the little guy. As an adult, you gave a voice to those who did not have one. May your love and legacy live forever.

I miss you, my friend.

MANY THANKS

This was an amazing collaborative effort and the following individuals have my eternal gratitude for their help, guidance, and support.

To God, for closing one door and opening up a bigger door and my heart to make this project happen.

To Carter, for your endless love, for being my rock, and letting me take this huge leap of faith.

To Aidan for "forcing" me to take some much needed breaks during this project to watch The Simpsons and laugh.

To my parents for Fortitude and Going and Getting.

To my in-laws for feeding us when I was neck deep in book deadlines.

To the Zen Den, for your support, comfort, letting me vent, and drying my tears.

To my Mindshare Tribe for helping me to dream big and see this project to fruition.

To the Job Accommodation Network (askjan.org) for not only their expertise they provided to this book, but also for their entire organization dedicated to helping individuals with all disabilities in the workplace.

To Emily Yee, for being the best editor in the world.

To Jennifer Covais, for being my Legal Eagle and researching the legal case studies.

Disclosure Policy:

All content and opinions are my own, and are not necessarily the opinions of anyone else mentioned in this book.

My friends at The Job Accommodation Network were a huge help in providing resources and information to this book. This is by no means an endorsement from askjan.org or the U.S. Department of Labor.

Disclaimer:

This book provides accurate information based on current research and I am sharing that advice with you. This information may change without the author's knowledge. It is not intended to provide health or legal guidelines or advice. I am not an attorney, doctor, or medical advisor. Please consult with your doctor and/or attorney before making any health or work-related changes. You are responsible for your actions or lack thereof. Pink Fortitude, LLC nor its owner are responsible or liable for your success or failure.

CONTENTS

MANAGING IN THE WORKPLACE

RESOURCES

STORIES FROM THE TRENCHES

CHAPTER 1
MY STORY

But first, let me share my experience with you.

In 2010, I was diagnosed with breast cancer. After nine months of surgery, chemotherapy, and radiation, the aggressive treatment was over. I thought I would start recovering, but instead, I kept getting sicker. One year later, I was diagnosed with Hashimoto's Thyroiditis, which is an autoimmune (AI) thyroid disease.

Even after the diagnosis and medication, I was not healing. My health plummeted. Every single day was a challenge of balancing chronic fatigue, migraines, joint pain, cognition issues, and constant diarrhea.

Five years later, I made some extreme lifestyle and dietary changes which immediately helped to improve my health. Unfortunately, there was cellular damage that was forbidding me from completely healing and my protocol needed to be amped up.

I had a six-figure salary working for a prestigious federal agency in Washington, DC. Earlier in the year, the management changed at my job, and not for the better. All of the stress compounded and my adrenals went to the red line. The Hashi's flare-up was the worst I had dealt with. My health was at a critical junction and I could barely function. I needed to focus on minimizing stress.

I had been doing the same job (more or less) with the same hours for approximately three years. While most people want to sleep in, I like getting up early, as it is the best part of my day, and I crash hard in the afternoon. Most days I need to take a nap or at least rest when I get home from work to give me energy to complete the day taking care of my family. The end goal would be for me to be able to quit my full time job, but at the time, it wasn't financially prudent. Despite making good money, we had medical bills and other financial obligations to take care of.

Our new management team came in like a wrecking ball. All around me, I saw how individuals would be targeted and was concerned that I would be next. A wise friend suggested that I get all of my paperwork up to date with the Equal Employment Opportunity (EEO) Office to stay ahead of the threat.

I found the paperwork which needed to be submitted, and I sent it to my doctor to complete. Several days later, my doctor contacted me and asked if I could provide some sample language to help her complete the form for my specific needs. This was obstacle number one. While we are all different, I couldn't find sample language anywhere to even help me get started.

I sent the sample language to my doctor, and when I received the paperwork back, I immediately submitted it to our EEO Office to apply for a reasonable accommodation of flexible hours and relatively low stress assignments. This was basically what I was already doing; I just wanted it documented and didn't want it to change because it was working for me, it was giving me the best productivity at work, and it was the best situation for my health.

All of my previous mangers before had been willing to work with me. I was working for a prestigious federal agency and I loved being a part of the mission. I want to work hard, but there are days that the AI gets the best of me, and I need a little bit of flexibility and understanding. I wasn't asking for much. My current managers were aware of my situation, but I could see the writing on the wall.

My new supervisor (of two weeks) cornered me as I was leaving to go home for a holiday weekend and without any kind of warning, told me that my hours would be changing by a two hour shift.

It was President's Day weekend, so we had a three day weekend. Normally something to be excited for, but the stress and shock hit my adrenals hard and I was sick all weekend, came down with a sinus infection, and was out of work for a portion of the following week.

Changing my hours by two hours may seem trivial to some. But for me, these hours were critical for my productivity at work and also for my overall health and well-being. I'm most productive early in the morning which is the best time to get my work done. And I need to nap in the afternoon when I get home.

This two hour shift change also increased my commuting time into and out of Washington, DC. My 20 minute morning commute was now 45 minutes. My 30 minute evening commute turned into an hour to an hour and a half with the city traffic. So now, I'm crashing at work, driving home praying that I don't fall asleep at the wheel during a long, stressful traffic-filled commute, and I'm unable to take an afternoon nap and rest when I get home because it's now time for dinner.

Allegedly, my hours were being changed due to a new "policy." But there was nothing in writing nor any kind of announcement. In fact, we had just had an All-Hands with our entire section and there was no mention about this policy or hours. The core hours of the agency were only a 30 minute difference than what I had been currently working. I spoke to my manager about a compromise to meet those core hours, but they were firm with the two hour shift.

It was now three weeks since my reasonable accommodation had been filed and I haven't heard anything. I figured out how to file the EEO claim and followed up with the reasonable accommodation office (RAO) coordinator, again, to no response.

I did hear back from the Family and Medical Leave Act (FMLA) office. The nurse in charge of my case responded, "I have Hashimoto's too. Why can't you just take some Synthroid and be fine? I take Synthroid and I don't have any issues." Wow. This is a nurse. In charge of FMLA. To say I was appalled at her insensitivity is an understatement.

When I spoke of my situation to my manager, I was extremely gracious in that I said I loved working in the unit and didn't want to leave, but that the new hours were not going to work with my health. I asked her for help in either a temporary assignment or finding another position in the division, or some kind of flexibility. She stood firm and was not willing to help. I assured her that if my work duties necessitated, that I would stay late to cover. But nothing would change her stance.

If the signs and clues weren't enough, I found out some more information. A colleague of mine in the same unit had chronic pain issues. I was not aware of the specifics of his case, condition, or accommodations. But I found out that my manager allowed him to work at an alternate work site, with flexible hours, and also gave him a laptop to be able to do work from home, which was actually pretty rare for my agency.

I think the world of this colleague and was glad that they were able to make arrangements for him. Please don't think I was mad at him or anything like that. I am simply using this as yet another example of how my management discriminated against me, and against the invisible illness known as AI.

I met a second time with the FMLA nurse and she reviewed my case. She took copious notes and assured me that everything will be fine and that my FMLA paperwork would go through. And it did.

Due to the increased stress throughout this whole process, I came down with an ear infection. I got dizzy and passed out at home. My husband was adamant about taking me to the emergency room, but I insisted I was fine. In hindsight, I wasn't fine. My body was shutting down, and I really should have gone to the hospital. I missed several more days of work.

I was scared to death. I was scared that any increased stress would send me to the hospital with full on adrenal failure. I was scared because my work was suffering. We were not in a secure enough position financially for me to resign. I could barely function at work. I could barely function at home. As the woman who used to be able to do it all, I now felt insignificant in all aspects of my life. Not to mention feeling ashamed, alone, and completely humiliated.

While my husband is extremely supportive, everything combined and compounded caused strife and stress in our marriage. I was stuck. I was scared. I felt alone. I didn't know what to do.

In the meantime, and because my condition kept worsening, my doctor strongly suggested I start an IV therapy to help manage my increasingly worse symptoms and flare-ups. This would require a visit to the office once a week, and since I *finally* had the FMLA approved at 480 hours of leave for the year, I was good to go. Or so I thought.

When I came back to the office, my manager didn't say hello or ask how I was. The first thing out of her mouth was, "Per your FMLA, you are only allowed to be sick two times per month with a duration of one to three days per episode. So you need to provide additional medical documentation for every day you were out sick."

I was bullied as a child, and I felt like I was back in the playground at my elementary school. Only this time, the bully was my boss. Someone who I was supposed to respect. I felt like I had no voice. I felt trapped with no way out.

I contacted the FMLA nurse and she assured me that was not the case, and my FMLA was covered. In line with federal guidelines, my doctor had given estimations of my flare-ups, and the FMLA office wrote "estimated" into their documentation. That was not good enough for my manager. She then contacted the head of FMLA to complain about my absences. One week later, I received a notice that my original FMLA was rescinded and I needed to start from square one and provide additional documentation to re-submit the paperwork. This also meant that I was not covered for the leave for the IV treatments until the new FMLA paperwork was approved.

I was shattered, and broke down into uncontrollable tears. My dear colleague walked me outside of the office space and into the stairwell. I sobbed for 30 straight minutes. Even going through cancer, I had never felt so helpless in my life. She sat quietly beside me and rubbed my back.

At some point in the middle of my breakdown, I felt a peace come over me. I knew that just like cancer, this was a trial that I had to go through. I knew God had a plan for me. I knew that I was called to find my fortitude and in turn help others through their journeys. I knew the road would be difficult and I didn't know what tomorrow would bring, but I had faith that everything would be ok.

"And we know that in all things God works for the good of those who love him and are called according to his purpose." – Romans 8:28

So, my friends, this is how it's done. The law states that you cannot be discriminated against. The law states that if you file a claim, you are protected from retribution. But management also has a way of being able to do whatever they want to do and it's all justified. This was how my agency pushes good people out. I wasn't the first. I won't be the last.

My story ends on a bittersweet note. My husband and I had some difficult discussions about me leaving my well-paying position of 13 years. There were many factors that we had to consider – my health, our finances, my teenaged Stepson, and our aging parents. It was a painful decision but we both agreed it would be the best one. I resigned.

I had several conversations with my attorney about the EEO claim. It was not my intent to be vengeful or spiteful. But I knew that if this happened to me, it will most certainly happen to others. And I don't ever want this to happen to someone else, especially someone struggling with AI.

The EEO claim went through the formal process, and it was decided that my situation did not meet the criteria for discrimination nor retribution. The agency's attorneys are only out to protect themselves, not to look out for their employees. Of course this is going to be their course of action, and they are going to make it an extremely difficult, painful, and expensive process to counter. After several conversations with my attorney, we decided not to pursue the case. But that didn't stop me from wanting to help others through the same situation.

In addition to being a cancer and autoimmune advocate, I'm now beginning to set up speaking engagements with agencies and companies to share how they can work with employees who have AI conditions. I've always been a firm believer to take whatever situation life hands you, and turn it around to help others.

This is how this book came to be.

CHAPTER 2
SURVIVOR STORIES

I wanted to share two additional stories with you. We all have different circumstances and conditions and regardless of the place you are in, please know that you are not alone.

Abby's Story

"Abby" (who ironically works for the health department) has been fighting her employer for the last 10 years with FMLA and accommodations for her chronic illness. She has managed to soldier through the ebbs and flows of both supportive and unsupportive management. After she was approved to periodically work from home, management then denied her request and moved her to an unfavorable environment, basically an environment that went against everything provided in her documentation and health records.

She filed a lawsuit but then had a change of heart and dropped it. Her management then wrote her up for abusing her FMLA, but due to her diligent documentation and the threat of a lawsuit, they dropped it. She loves her job, and has faith that an understanding supervisor will eventually be hired.

Rebecca's Story

"Rebecca" has fibromyalgia and arthritis and works for a well-known telecommunications company. She worked with her supervisor, manager, and HR to explain her condition and set up accommodations. When she has a flare-up, her managers go out of their way to work with her to provide her whatever she needs. HR even worked as a liaison between her and the insurance company.

YOUR LEGAL RIGHTS

CHAPTER 3
IS AUTOIMMUNE DISEASE A DISABILITY?

This is the million dollar question. The short answer is that if your autoimmune disease causes certain conditions under the Americans with Disability Act, then yes, you are protected under the law.

The long answer is that it's a lot more complicated. First of all, I can't tell you how many individuals I've spoken with who have AI, who do not view having an autoimmune disease as a disability. Some of them have been able to manage their conditions and live productive lives without any issues. Some of them are too proud to consider themselves disabled.

It's a double edged sword. I think the word "disability" sometimes has negative connotations in our society of someone who is not able to perform or function. One of the challenges of having AI is the common occurrence of people saying, "But you don't look sick." If you are able to hold down a full time job, but still need some accommodations, your manager or company may not understand the connection. Or you may not view yourself as having a disability, especially compared to someone else with a more visible disability.

It's a change in mindset and education. The purpose of this book is not to tell you to give up and become a victim. The purpose of this book is to empower you with knowledge so that you can rise above your illness and challenges and thrive both at home and in the workplace.

Back to the law. We will get into many more legal details throughout this entire section. But I wanted to address the most important question first – is Autoimmune Disease a disability?

The ADA was amended in 2008, and went into effect January 1, 2009. If AI was ever blurry under the law before, these amendments added a new category of major life activities called "major bodily functions," which specifically includes the endocrine and immune systems.

According to this Amendment, under Section 4, Disability Defined and Rules of Construction, (2) Major Life Activities, (B) Major Bodily Functions, it states, "For purposes of paragraph (1), a major life activity also includes the operation of a major bodily function, including but not limited to, functions of the immune system, normal cell growth, digestive, bowel, bladder, neurological, brain, respiratory, circulatory, endocrine, and reproductive functions."

It doesn't matter how you feel about being considered disabled. It certainly doesn't matter if your employer wants to acknowledge your disability. The language of the law is crystal clear.

If you meet the required conditions under the law, then you are legally protected under the ADA.

"If you have a disability and are qualified to do a job, the ADA protects you from job discrimination on the basis of your disability." (www.ada.gov)

CHAPTER 4
YOUR RIGHTS IN THE WORKPLACE
101

The following is a brief summary of the protections that you are legally entitled to. We will delve further into each of these in the next section.

Americans with Disabilities Act

The Americans with Disabilities Act (ADA) prohibits discrimination in all employment practices against "qualified individuals with disabilities." This means that you cannot be eliminated from consideration for employment or from your job because of your disability if you have the skills, experience, education or other requirements for the job you already have or the job you want, and you can perform the essential functions of the position with or without reasonable accommodation.

U.S. Equal Employment Opportunity Commission

The U.S. Equal Employment Opportunity Commission (EEOC) is responsible for enforcing federal laws that make it illegal to discriminate against a job applicant or an employee because of the person's race, color, religion, sex (including pregnancy), national origin, age (40 or older), disability or genetic information. It is also illegal to discriminate against a person because the person complained about discrimination, filed a charge of discrimination, or participated in an employment discrimination investigation or lawsuit.

Family and Medical Leave Act

The Family and Medical Leave Act (FMLA) allows employees working for a company with more than 50 employees a job-protected leave for specified family and medical reasons, including:

- Caring for the employee's spouse, child or parent who has a serious health condition
- A serious health condition that makes the employee unable to perform the essential functions of their job.

Reasonable Accommodations

A reasonable accommodation is a modification or adjustment in the work environment that enables a qualified individual with a disability to enjoy an equal employment opportunity.

CHAPTER 5
AMERICANS WITH DISABILITY ACT

Due to the nature of this specific legal information, all information in this section was taken directly and verbatim from the Americans with Disability Act and the U.S. Equal Employment Opportunity Commission:

- www.ada.gov
- https://www.eeoc.gov/facts/ada18.html
- https://www.ada.gov/cguide.htm

The Americans with Disabilities Act of 1990 (ADA) makes it unlawful to discriminate in employment against a qualified individual with a disability. The ADA also outlaws discrimination against individuals with disabilities in State and local government services, public accommodations, transportation and telecommunications.

According to the ADA, a disability is:
- A physical or mental impairment that substantially limits one or more major life activities of an individual
- A record of such an impairment
- Being regarded as having such impairment.

This law is enforced by the U.S. Equal Employment Opportunity Commission and State and local civil rights enforcement agencies that work with the Commission.

Job discrimination against people with disabilities is illegal if practiced by:

- Private employers
- State and local governments
- Employment agencies
- Labor organizations
- Labor-management committees.

The part of the ADA enforced by the EEOC outlaws job discrimination by:

- All employers, including State and local government employers, with 25 or more employees after July 26, 1992
- All employers, including State and local government employers, with 15 or more employees after July 26, 1994.

Another part of the ADA, enforced by the U.S. Department of Justice, prohibits discrimination in State and local government programs and activities, including discrimination by all State and local governments, regardless of the number of employees, after January 26, 1992.

Because the ADA establishes overlapping responsibilities in both EEOC and DOJ for employment by State and local governments, the Federal enforcement effort is coordinated by EEOC and DOJ to avoid duplication in investigative and enforcement activities. In addition, since some private and governmental employers are already covered by nondiscrimination and affirmative action requirements under the Rehabilitation Act of 1973, EEOC, DOJ, and the Department of Labor similarly coordinate the enforcement effort under the ADA and the Rehabilitation Act.

If you have a disability and are qualified to do a job, the ADA protects you from job discrimination on the basis of your disability. Under the ADA, you have a disability if you have a physical or mental impairment that substantially limits a major life activity. The ADA also protects you if you have a history of such a disability, or if an employer believes that you have such a disability, even if you don't.

To be protected under the ADA, you must have, have a record of, or be regarded as having a substantial, as opposed to a minor, impairment. A substantial impairment is one that significantly limits or restricts a major life activity such as hearing, seeing, speaking, walking, breathing, performing manual tasks, caring for oneself, learning or working.

The ADA makes it unlawful to discriminate in all employment practices such as:

- Recruitment
- Firing
- Hiring
- Training
- Job assignments
- Promotions
- Pay
- Benefits
- Lay off
- Leave
- All other employment related activities.

It is also unlawful for an employer to retaliate against you for asserting your rights under the ADA. The Act also protects you if you are a victim of discrimination because of your family, business, social or other relationship or association with an individual with a disability.

If you have a disability, you must also be qualified to perform the essential functions or duties of a job, with or without reasonable accommodation, in order to be protected from job discrimination by the ADA. This means two things.

First, you must satisfy the employer's requirements for the job, such as education, employment experience, skills or licenses.

Second, you must be able to perform the essential functions of the job with or without reasonable accommodation. Essential functions are the fundamental job duties that you must be able to perform on your own or with the help of a reasonable accommodation. An employer cannot refuse to hire you because your disability prevents you from performing duties that are not essential to the job.

CHAPTER 6
DEFINITION OF DISABILITY AND DISABILITY DISCRIMINATION

Due to the nature of this specific legal information, all information in this section was taken directly and verbatim from the U.S. Equal Employment Opportunity Commission and U.S. Department of Justice:

- https://www.eeoc.gov/eeoc/index.cfm
- https://www.eeoc.gov/laws/types/disability.cfm
- https://www.justice.gov/crt/disability-rights-section

Not everyone with a medical condition is protected by the law. In order to be protected, a person must be qualified for the job and have a disability as defined by the law.

A person can show that he or she has a disability in one of three ways:

- A person may be disabled if he or she has a physical or mental condition that substantially limits a major life activity (such as walking, talking, seeing, hearing, or learning).

- A person may be disabled if he or she has a history of a disability (such as cancer that is in remission).
- A person may be disabled if he is believed to have a physical or mental impairment that is not transitory (lasting or expected to last six months or less) and minor (even if he does not have such an impairment).

Disability discrimination occurs when an employer or other entity covered by the Americans with Disabilities Act, as amended, or the Rehabilitation Act, as amended, treats a qualified individual with a disability who is an employee or applicant unfavorably because she has a disability.

Disability discrimination also occurs when a covered employer or other entity treats an applicant or employee less favorably because she has a history of a disability (such as cancer that is controlled or in remission) or because she is believed to have a physical or mental impairment that is not transitory (lasting or expected to last six months or less) and minor (even if she does not have such an impairment).

The law requires an employer to provide reasonable accommodation to an employee or job applicant with a disability, unless doing so would cause significant difficulty or expense for the employer ("undue hardship").

The law also protects people from discrimination based on their relationship with a person with a disability (even if they do not themselves have a disability). For example, it is illegal to discriminate against an employee because her husband has a disability.

.

CHAPTER 7
FAMILY AND MEDICAL LEAVE ACT

Due to the nature of this specific legal information, all information in this section was taken directly and verbatim from the U.S. Department of Labor: https://www.dol.gov/whd/fmla/

The FMLA entitles eligible employees of covered employers to take unpaid, job-protected leave for specified family and medical reasons with continuation of group health insurance coverage under the same terms and conditions as if the employee had not taken leave. Eligible employees are entitled to:

- Twelve workweeks of leave in a 12-month period for the birth of a child and to care for the newborn child within one year of birth
- The placement with the employee of a child for adoption or foster care and to care for the newly placed child within one year of placement
- To care for the employee's spouse, child, or parent who has a serious health condition

- A serious health condition that makes the employee unable to perform the essential functions of his or her job
- Any qualifying exigency arising out of the fact that the employee's spouse, son, daughter, or parent is a covered military member on "covered active duty"
- Twenty-six workweeks of leave during a single 12-month period to care for a covered service member with a serious injury or illness if the eligible employee is the service member's spouse, son, daughter, parent, or next of kin (military caregiver leave).

If your employer requests medical certification, you only have 15 calendar days to provide it in most circumstances. You are responsible for the cost of getting the certification from a health care provider and for making sure that the certification is provided to your employer. If you fail to provide the requested medical certification, your FMLA leave may be denied. The medical certification must include some specific information, including:

- Contact information for the health care provider
- When the serious health condition began
- How long the condition is expected to last
- Appropriate medical facts about the condition (which may include information on symptoms, hospitalization, doctors visits, and referrals for treatment)
- Whether you are unable to work or your family member is in need of care

- Whether you need leave continuously or intermittently. (If you need to take leave a little bit at a time, the certification should include an estimate of how much time you will need for each absence, how often you will be absent, and information establishing the medical necessity for taking such intermittent leave.)

The U.S. Department of Labor's Wage and Hour Division (WHD) is responsible for administering and enforcing the Family and Medical Leave Act for most employees.

If you have questions, or you think that your rights under the FMLA may have been violated, you can contact WHD at 1-866-487-9243. You will be directed to the WHD office nearest you for assistance. There are over 200 WHD offices throughout the country staffed with trained professionals to help you.

The information below is useful when filing a complaint with WHD:

- Your name
- Your address and phone number (how you can be contacted)
- The name of the company where you work or worked
- Location of the company (this may be different than the actual job site where you worked)
- Phone number of the company
- Manager or owner's name
- The circumstances of your FMLA request and your employer's response.

Your employer is prohibited from interfering with, restraining, or denying the exercise of FMLA rights, retaliating against you for filing a complaint and cooperating with the Wage and Hour Division, or bringing a private action to court. You should contact the Wage and Hour Division immediately if your employer retaliates against you for engaging in any of these legally protected activities.

CHAPTER 8
DISABILITY DISCRIMINATION AND REASONABLE ACCOMMODATION

Due to the nature of this specific legal information, all information in this section was taken directly and verbatim from the U.S. Equal Employment Opportunity Commission:

- www.eeoc.gov/policy/docs/accommodation.html
- https://www.eeoc.gov/facts/ada18.html

The law requires an employer to provide reasonable accommodation to an employee or job applicant with a disability, unless doing so would cause significant difficulty or expense for the employer.

A reasonable accommodation is any change in the work environment (or in the way things are usually done) to help a person with a disability apply for a job, perform the duties of a job, or enjoy the benefits and privileges of employment.

Reasonable accommodation might include, for example, making the workplace accessible for wheelchair users or providing a reader or interpreter for someone who is blind or hearing impaired.

An employer is required to provide a reasonable accommodation to a qualified applicant or employee with a disability unless the employer can show that the accommodation would be an undue hardship -- that is, that it would require significant difficulty or expense. Undue hardship means that the accommodation would be too difficult or too expensive to provide, in light of the employer's size, financial resources, and the needs of the business.

An employer may not refuse to provide an accommodation just because it involves some cost. An employer does not have to provide the exact accommodation the employee or job applicant wants. If more than one accommodation works, the employer may choose which one to provide.

THE WORST CASE SCENARIO - DISCRIMINATION

The following section discusses the worst case scenario – discrimination and the legal system. It is not meant to scare you, to be negative, or to project a broken system. It's meant to give you a complete view of the situation and real life information, which may not be what you want to hear. Life is not always rainbows and puppy kisses and I would be giving you a disservice and incomplete information without this section.

Sometimes things work out; sometimes they don't. This is real life, and sometimes the harsh realities we have to face with autoimmune conditions. The laws are there to protect us, but sometimes, reality doesn't always cooperate. This section was purposely placed in the middle of the book, because I did not want to end on a negative note.

Let's hope that you will never have to face the worst case scenario. Read through this section to give you the other side of the conversation. The book will then finish in the final section with positive, actionable steps you can take to make your situation better, and resources to further educate and help you.

CHAPTER 9
LEGAL CASE STUDIES

McNary v. Schreiber Foods, Inc.
Decided August 1, 2008
Smith, Levenski R. "FindLaw's United States Eighth Circuit Case and Opinions." *Findlaw.* N.p., n.d. Web. 20 July 2017.

In 2008, a case is argued before the Eighth Circuit Court of Appeals in which David McNary of Springfield, Missouri sued Schreiber Foods Incorporated for wrongful termination of employment in violation of the Americans with Disabilities Act (42 U.S. Code § 12101).

The district court ruled in favor of Schreiber Foods, and the Circuit Court affirmed the decision of the lower court.

McNary, who suffers from Graves disease and Diabetes, was employed with Schreiber Foods, a dairy product distributor, from 1978 until 2005 when he was terminated. From 1999 until his termination he worked in the sanitation department. According to McNary, he made his coworkers and supervisors aware of his need for breaks and periods of rest due to the limitations his illness presented him with. McNary's physician however, stated that McNary could work without any restrictions or accommodation.

On September 22, 2005, McNary came into work to clean the wet and dry trash compactors. Not long after initiating the task he felt dizzy and lightheaded. He left the compactors, and went into another room where he sat down, put his feet up and closed his eyes. McNary claims that he was simply resting his eyes and legs as he was in pain and was not sleeping. His two supervisors walked into the room when they believed McNary to be sound asleep.

The two supervisors returned to the room about fifteen minutes later to find McNary in the same position. They asked McNary if he was asleep, and McNary responded saying that he was not asleep, but enduring severe eye pain. His two supervisors, Johnston and Swarnes, submitted a Corrective Action Form to management, which led to a 5 day suspension, followed by his eventual termination.

In January of 2006, McNary filed a complaint against Schreiber Foods alleging that the company discriminated against him due to his disease, thus violating the ADA. The district court ruled that Schreiber Foods had provided legitimate and nondiscriminatory reasoning for McNary's termination. When the Circuit Court heard the case, they affirmed the lower court's decision for the following reason.

In order for a plaintiff to prevail in proving that the employer was in fact discriminating against the plaintiff, they have to prove the employers reasoning for termination was a pretext of discrimination. To do this, a plaintiff must show sufficient evidence to prove a motive for the discrimination at hand that rest behind the false reasoning for termination. In this case, McNary would have to prove that the company fired him not for an unauthorized break, but for the want to dismiss him solely because of his disability.

Moreover, the court affirmed this decision for the fact that McNary could not provide enough evidence to support the claim that Schreiber Foods had in fact discriminated against him. The company provided legitimate and just reasoning for McNary's termination that coincides within the guidelines of the ADA.

Zana Griffith v. Boise Cascade, INC

Decided May 2, 2002
Sweeney, Dennis J. "FindLaw's Court of Appeals of Washington Case and Opinions." *Findlaw*. N.p., n.d. Web. 22 July 2017.

In July of 1989, Zana Griffith was hired as an extraboard for Boise Cascade. An extraboard is a position in which employees fill temporary vacancies in various departments. The position can include physical labor. The position entailed continuous standing, sometimes for an entire shift. Griffith belonged to a union which required seniority for job reassignment.

In July 1994, Griffith contracted Chicken Pox. Her doctor anticipated Griffith to be fully recovered in six to ten days, however, Griffith soon experienced muscle pains and difficulty sleeping. Ms. Griffith was diagnosed with polymyositis the following November. Polymyositis is an autoimmune disease that causes chronic muscle pain and weakness. Her doctor suggested that she switch to desk work so that she could rest her muscles, which consequently led her to leave her job. She was out of work for the remainder of 1994, until her doctor allowed her to return to work in the following January with restrictions.

Boise Cascade had determined that Ms. Griffith was unable to perform the essentials of the extraboard job with or without accommodations. There were no compatible positions available for Ms. Griffith that coincided with her level of seniority, so she was left off of work.

On August 22, 1995, Griffith met with Boise Cascade for a physical evaluation in which the evaluation scored Griffith at "least amount of physical activity recommended". No compatible positions were available for her, so she remained out of work. Ms. Griffith then filed a discrimination claim with the Washington Human Rights Commission.

Boise responded that they were indeed trying to accommodate her, and its first step was to try to accommodate the employee within the position, and then try to find the employee another available position. Griffith returned back to the position in October 1995. A position opened up in January 1996, however Griffith's doctor said that she could not handle the requirements of the position safely, so Boise did not offer her the position but offered her an alternate position instead. The job allowed for her to stay seated the entire shift, but Griffith declined the offer because it did not coincide with her long term career goals.

On April 2nd, 1996, Boise informed Griffith that it would no longer accommodate her condition as an extraboard for the company. On April 7th, 1998, Boise finally terminated Griffith after a collective bargaining agreement.

Griffith sued Boise for emotional distress, handicap discrimination, and violation of public policy. The trial court granted review of the case and dismissed the charges against Boise. After review from the Washington Court of Appeals, the court affirms the trial court's decision.

The first question the court looked to answer is if the company reasonably accommodated an employee with a disability. In order to have successfully done so, the company needs to have affirmatively taken steps to help the employee keep their current position through accommodations, or offering other positions to the disabled employee. The court has decided that Boise had taken all the necessary steps to successfully do so.

Griffith argues that Boise Cascade violated public policy, because the company allegedly acted in a manner inconsistent with a Washington law that prohibited discrimination in the workplace of any kind, similar to that of the ADA. The court dismissed this charge because again, Boise reasonably accommodated Griffith in accordance to the act.

Therefore, the district court properly dismissed Griffith's claims of violation of public policy, thus resulting in the circuit court affirming the lower court's decision.

CHAPTER 10
WHAT DO I DO IF I THINK I'M BEING DISCRIMINATED AGAINST?

If you think you have been discriminated against in employment on the basis of disability after July 26, 1992, you should contact the U.S. Equal Employment Opportunity Commission. A charge of discrimination generally must be filed within 180 days of the alleged discrimination. You may have up to 300 days to file a charge if there is a State or local law that provides relief for discrimination on the basis of disability. However, to protect your rights, it is best to contact EEOC promptly if discrimination is suspected.

You may file a charge of discrimination on the basis of disability by contacting any EEOC field office, located in cities throughout the United States. If you have been discriminated against, you are entitled to a remedy that will place you in the position you would have been in if the discrimination had never occurred. You may be entitled to hiring, promotion, reinstatement, back pay, or reasonable accommodation, including reassignment. You may also be entitled to attorney's fees.

While the EEOC can only process ADA charges based on actions occurring on or after July 26, 1992, you may already be protected by State or local laws or by other current federal laws. EEOC field offices can refer you to the agencies that enforce those laws.

To contact the EEOC, look in your telephone directory under "U.S. Government." For information and instructions on reaching your local office, call:

- (800) 669-4000 (Voice)
- (800) 669-6820 (TDD)
- In the Washington, D.C. 202 Area Code, call 202-663-4900 (voice) or 202-663-4494 (TDD).

Keep a written record of every single conversation and email that could be used for or against your case. The total amount of paperwork that I accumulated was about six inches high over the course of four months. I was meticulous. If I had gone forth with the EEO case, I would have needed this documentation.

Keep a notebook dedicated to your condition and case. Keep a file of all documentation. If you send an email, cc or bcc yourself for record. Keep records of all communications, both written and verbal. Try to have a witness if possible. If you have a conversation with your supervisor, take notes, and if it makes sense, have someone else in the room with you to be a witness of the conversation.

Get witnesses. If someone in your office witnesses a conversation, write down the date, time, location, and individuals involved.

At home, keep a copy of all of your medical records and lab results.

There are always going to be awesome managers who are supportive. There are always going to be the knuckleheads that don't get it. People are people. Don't take it personally.

CHAPTER 11
THE HARSH REALITY

Working for an awesome manager is the holy grail of the work environment. Working for an unsupportive boss will kill your soul.

The burden of proof is on you to prove you were being discriminated against. It will cost you a lot of time and money and stress. I mentioned the six inches of documentation I meticulously kept. I also had to pay out $2,000 in retainer fees. Do you have that kind of money to pay out to pursue a case? Do you have those kind of organization skills to keep well documented paperwork? Do you have the bandwidth for that amount of time and stress?

I was informed by an unnamed government official that their particular agency uses the "Jerk Management Defense" to win the majority of their discrimination cases. The organization will only look out for the best interests of the organization. You may have everything documented and an awesome attorney ready to rumble, but the Jerk Management Defense wins cases. You weren't being discriminated against. Your boss is simply a jerk. The "needs of the organization" is another popular defense that is extremely difficult to win against.

People are people, no matter where you are. A good manager will be understanding and a bad manager can be vindictive. In all honesty, an unfavorable environment is more likely to become worse instead of better, even despite the laws which protect you.

Have a backup plan, and don't be afraid to look for another job within your company or at a completely different company. Always keep your resume up to date. Sock away as much money as you can to give yourself and family as much extra financial stability in case you have some difficult decisions to make.

As I stated earlier and it bears repeating, practice stress reduction activities and take care of yourself. Eat healthy and exercise, meditate, go to church, pray, take a bath, talk with friends. Arm yourself with as much ammunition as you can during this process and rely on your support system.

Talk to your family and ask for help. My husband took over some of my home responsibilities and my stepson even pitched in to help. I remember coming home late one night after an exhausting day and commute home and barely making it through the front door and my husband had cooked dinner and my stepson was washing the dishes. It was great to have them step up and help.

Finally, stay positive. Find your inner peace through the turmoil and know in your heart that everything will work out. Even in the toughest of situations, there is always good to be found.

Yes, there have been discrimination cases where the individual with a disability won. I personally applaud anyone who has the grit to take these cases to trial. They are expensive and exhausting, but they do make a difference. I chose to not litigate. It was the best decision for myself and my family. Instead, I wrote this book to share my experience with you to help you become empowered to make your situation better.

MANAGING <u>YOUR</u> CONDITION IN THE WORKPLACE

CHAPTER 12
SHOULD I TELL MY EMPLOYER?

Should you notify your employer about your AI condition and disability? Unfortunately, we don't have a crystal ball to help us figure out the correct answer. I'm going to run through several scenarios that will help you to think through your answer, but the only one who can answer this question is you.

According to Tracie DeFreitas, MS, CLMS, Lead Consultant, ADA Specialist at the Job Accommodation Network (JAN), "Deciding if, when, and how to share disability-related information with a prospective or current employer can be overwhelming."

DeFreitas continues, "The decision-making process requires answering a number of personal questions that may be different in each employment experience. There is no single right or wrong approach to disclosing information about your medical impairment. The process can include questions like: 'Do I have an obligation to disclose?' 'When is the right time?' 'How much information does the employer need?' and 'How will disclosing the information affect my employment?'

"Generally there is no obligation to disclose disability-related information to an employer *until the need for reasonable accommodation becomes apparent.* Disability disclosure can occur during any stage of the employment process, including pre-employment, post-offer, and while employed – whether it be within days, months, or years of initially being hired. Generally it is up to the individual with the disability to determine the right time to disclose, given their particular circumstances.

"Why disclose? Individuals will usually disclose their medical impairment when it becomes apparent that an accommodation is needed to perform essential job duties, to receive benefits or privileges of employment, or to explain an unusual circumstance, such as, when there is a disability-related performance issue, or when an individual is behaving in an unusual manner. The need to disclose or request accommodation will become evident when an individual knows there is a workplace barrier related to their medical impairment."

According to the Department of Labor, "The laws require that qualified applicants and employees with disabilities be provided with reasonable accommodations. Yet, in order to benefit from the ADA and the Rehabilitation Act, you must disclose your disability. An employer is only required to provide work-related accommodations if you disclose your disability to the appropriate individuals."

Keep in mind that once the information is out about your disability, you can't put the toothpaste back into the tube. It seems like life these days isn't meant for secrets. If your co-workers know about your condition, even if they are trusted in discretion, what happens if they inadvertently say something while the boss is in listening distance? Are you posting about your illness on social media? Even if you decide not to tell your employer, there are no guarantees that they won't find out.

Individuals with AI are in a unique position as most of our symptoms are invisible. No one can see how much you are suffering, and unless you say something, they will never be aware. What if you are having bouts of extreme fatigue or cognition issues? It is possible that your work may be affected. Would you prefer to get written up for your work performance? Or disclose? Because most AI conditions and symptoms are invisible, what if your employer or manager doesn't believe you? What if your co-workers think you are just being lazy or making excuses for not working hard?

Let's say you decide not to tell your employer because you fear it will compromise your job. If your manager finds out, and they are not legally allowed to say anything to you. But now, all of a sudden, they may be doing little things to make your life miserable. Your work comes back extra scrutinized. You now have to account for your time in and out of the office on every single break. If you feel they are discriminating against you because of your disability, you have no documentation and nothing to prove your case.

According to the Department of Labor, as a person with a disability, you have these protections and responsibilities when it comes to disclosure:

You are entitled to:
- Have information about your disability treated confidentially and respectfully
- Seek information about hiring practices from any organization
- Choose to disclose your disability at any time during the employment process
- Receive reasonable accommodations for an interview

- Be considered for a position based on your skill and merit
- Have respectful questioning about your disability for the purpose of determining whether you need accommodations and if so, what kind.

You have the responsibility to:
- Disclose your need for any work-related reasonable accommodations
- Bring your skills and merits to the table
- Be truthful, self-determined, and proactive.

JAN offers some additional tips to keep in mind:
- The timing of a request can be rather important. It's not necessary to disclose a disability if sharing the information will have no impact on the employment situation. If an accommodation is not needed, it's probably not necessary to disclose a hidden disability that will have no impact on job performance.
- While early disclosure may not be necessary, it is suggested that individuals disclose their medical impairment and request accommodation before job performance suffers or conduct problems occur. According to the EEOC, an employer does not have to rescind discipline (including a termination) or an evaluation warranted by poor performance simply because an employee has disclosed a disability or requested accommodation (EEOC, 2008).
- JAN offers a number of resources related to the topic of disability disclosure. To learn more, visit Accommodation Information by Topic: A to Z at jan.org.

CHAPTER 13
REASONABLE ACCOMMODATIONS
FOR AUTOIMMUNE CONDITIONS

Two very common symptoms across many with AI are fatigue and joint pain, both of which are "invisible." It is ironic that the accommodations for visible disabilities such as mobility, blindness, or deafness typically require costs for ramps, interpreters, or readers, while the first line of accommodations for individuals with AI such as flexible hours, flexible breaks, or working from home do not require a cost to the employer, but can sometimes be more difficult to obtain.

This statement is in no way meant to say that one disability is any better or worse than another, but more to let you know that what can seem like a simple process may be a simple process, or actually end up being an uphill battle. Employers need to take **ALL** disabilities seriously, regardless of how obvious and visible (or not) they may be.

For those struggling with fatigue, accommodations might include extra rest periods, reduced hours or the ability to work at home. Your life is not just about your work, and you only have so much energy to expend on any given day. You still need to function during those 16 hours of the day that you are not at your job. Conserving energy is crucial.

According to JAN, there is no comprehensive list of accommodations that MUST be provided under the ADA. While all AI diseases and symptoms are different, this is a substantial list of reasonable accommodations to help get you started. It is by no means a complete list, but I've compiled accommodations that are specific to help those with AI.

Common Accommodations:
- Work from home
- Allow flexible work and leave schedule
- Allow periodic and/or longer breaks
- Reduce job stress
- Reduce or eliminate physical exertion
- Provide parking close to work site
- Switch to an ergonomic chair
- Keep work environment free from dust, smoke, odor, and fumes
- Implement a "fragrance-free" workplace policy and a "smoke free" building policy
- Avoid temperature extremes
- Use fan/air-conditioner or heater at the workstation
- Redirect air conditioning and heating vents
- Provide sensitivity training to coworkers
- Allow telephone calls during work hours to doctors and others for support
- Provide information on counseling and employee assistance programs
- Restructure job to only include essential functions
- Control glare by adding a glare screen to the computer.

Additional Accommodations:

- Allow use of a service animal at work
- Move workstation closer to the restroom
- Provide access to a refrigerator
- Allow for workstation to minimize distractions
- Provide written job instructions when possible
- Allow a self-paced workload
- Provide ergonomic workstation
- Provide scooter or mobility aid
- Provide arm supports
- Install automatic door openers
- Modify the workstation to make it accessible
- Adjust desk height if wheelchair or scooter is used
- Install low wattage overhead lights
- Replace fluorescent lighting with LED, halogen, or natural lighting
- Use computer monitor glare guards, adjust monitor intensity and color, and decrease the cursor speed of the mouse
- Avoid infectious agents and chemicals.

"When engaging in the interactive process for your accommodation, remember to be open-minded and creative," DeFreitas encourages.

CHAPTER 14
SAMPLE LANGUAGE

Every accommodation will be unique, and with the help of JAN, I've compiled some sample language to help you start drafting your accommodation request, along with links to help you with additional research.

Flexible Schedule

[Condition] causes [symptoms] [source]. A flexible schedule will help me to work optimally during hours of increased attentiveness. This schedule will also include periods of mental rest to help me refocus and reorient into my work.

Examples of a flexible schedule would be adjusting starting and ending times of the workday, combining regularly scheduled breaks to create one extended break or dividing large breaks into smaller segments, and allowing work to be completed during hours when the employee is most mentally alert. (askjan.org)

Modified Break Schedule

[Condition] causes [symptoms] [source]. Periodic rest breaks will help me to perform my job at the optimal level by providing time to rest, move, or stretch. Time used for these breaks can be taken from my currently provided break time or lunch time so there is not an impact on productivity.

Job Restructuring

[Condition] causes [symptoms] [source]. It is my request to restructure the following tasks [Task A, Task B] with [co-worker name]'s tasks [Task A, Task B].

Job restructuring is a form of reasonable accommodation which enables many qualified individuals with disabilities to perform jobs effectively. Job restructuring as a reasonable accommodation may involve reallocating or redistributing the marginal functions of a job. However, an employer is not required to reallocate essential functions of a job as a reasonable accommodation. Essential functions, by definition, are those that a qualified individual must perform, with or without an accommodation. (askjan.org)

An employer may exchange marginal functions of a job that cannot be performed by a person with a disability for marginal job functions performed by one or more other employees. Although an employer is not required to reallocate essential job functions, it may be a reasonable accommodation to modify the essential functions of a job by changing when or how they are done. (askjan.org)

Telework, Work from Home, Working Remotely

[Condition] causes [symptoms] [source]. By working from home [during these days of the week, during inclement weather, etc] will ensure that I will complete my job and tasks without missing work.

Telework, within certain fields, can be an excellent alternative for employees who have conditions that make it difficult for them to leave their home or reliably travel to a place of work. Employers should consider if a job can be made compatible with telework for their employees and communicate their expectations and requirement for the job to be performed out of home. Allowing work from home during worksite or office construction; extremely hot, cold, or inclement weather; or parking renovations could be a reasonable accommodation. (askjan.org)

Ergonomic and Adjustable Office Chairs

[Condition] causes [symptoms] [source]. By switching my office chair to an adjustable office chair, this will provide support to my joints and help to ease the pain during work hours.

Adjustable Workstations for Office Settings

[Condition] causes [symptoms] [source]. By switching to an adjustable workstation, this will allow for me to alternate between sitting and standing to help to ease the pain during work hours.

Stand/Lean Stools

[Condition] causes [symptoms] [source]. Because my job requires me to stand for a long period of time, switching to a stand/lean stool will help to support and stabilize my body and help to ease the pain during work hours.

Stand/lean stools are available to assist individuals who must stand or sit for long periods of time. Stand/lean stools allow an individual to adjust his/her positioning, relieve standing strain by leaning, and relieve sitting pressure by leaning. Stand/lean stools are useful for brief mini-breaks and allow an easy return to an upright position. Stand/lean stools give individuals the ability to work in an upright position with most of their weight resting on the padded seat. A stand/lean stool helps support the body in a standing position and stabilizes the body in an upright position, reducing back strain and minimizing leg fatigue. Some stools swivel and tilt, some have backrests, and some are made for industrial and office environments. (askjan.org)

Anti-Fatigue Matting

[Condition] causes [symptoms] [source]. Because my job requires me to stand for a long period of time, standing on an anti-fatigue mat will help to support and stabilize my body and help to ease the pain and fatigue during work hours.

CHAPTER 15
THE PROCESS, THE BOSS, AND A FEW PIECES OF ADVICE

<u>Do the Right Thing. Always.</u>
Locate your company's HR policy and be sure to follow the rules. ALWAYS do the right thing, and be "by the book". Do not give your employer a chance to retaliate. I was one of those employees who was always in a good mood, always positive, always asked to help others, and always did the right thing. One of my co-workers joked that I could come to work with my arm cut off and bleeding all over the floor and I would be like, "Oh look at the pretty red pattern it's making on the carpet!" I can't change who I am, nor should you change who you are. But please understand that it may be difficult for a manager to "believe" you are sick when you look fine and are a positive, productive, and helpful employee.

I had many years of understanding management. For six years, I was given different accommodations including a parking pass in the building, flexible hours, and flexible assignments. I had managers who went out of their way without the burden of paperwork to ensure that I was taken care of. In return, I did everything I could to be the best employee for them and help them as much as possible.

It was an unfortunate circumstance that one bad manager pushed me out. But I still treated her with respect and volunteered to help and worked as hard as I could. She even said to me how much she appreciated my positive attitude throughout the difficult situation. Whether you are in an ideal work situation or are dealing with a demanding boss, do the right thing. Always.

Do Your Homework

I asked my resources at JAN to help with this one. "Individuals with disabilities who understand the basic principles of the ADA going into employment will be able to leverage the legislation to – when necessary – ask for what is needed to enable success on the job. Know that accommodations may be possible. Making a small adjustment in the way things are usually done at work, can be a big game changer for someone who has limitations related to an autoimmune disorder. Come to the table with accommodation solutions and resources – like JAN. Be prepared with ideas, exhibit a collaborative spirit, and approach the situation with positive, effective solutions."

Filling out Forms

Do your research and find out what your employer's policies are. Find out all of the forms you need to fill out. Check, double check, ask and re-ask. I guarantee there will be more forms than you think you need. It's best to ensure you have all of the forms you need before you ask your doctor to complete them.

Once you have all of the forms, make several copies of the blank form. Keep one blank copy and fill out the information on a second copy. Give both copies to your doctor to complete. The doctor may want to use their own language, but providing sample language will be very helpful. And then, make copies of the completed forms for your own records.

Also, be cognizant of your deadlines, if any. Be sure to give your physician ample time to complete the forms so that you can submit them in a timely manner.

Let me re-state to make copies of everything. I received several phone calls and emails from the HR/EEO units I was working with at my agency, because "I did not submit all of the paperwork". I was able to quickly respond, "Yes, I did. On this day, with this person, and here is the scanned copy of the 50 pages for your record."

I'm not sure why or how my agency's HR/EEO employees can be so flippant to lose important medical records with personal information, but it happens all of the time. And oh by the way, the information on these forms is both HIPPA (Health Insurance Portability and Accountability Act) and PII (Personal Identifiable Information), which is legally protected. You have rights.

Communicate with the Boss

Once you know your organization's process and you have the forms (if any) to fill out, you will need to communicate with your supervisor or manager. We all have different personalities. Queue into your boss. Is she chatty? Does he want you to get right to the point?

Just like if you were to ask for a raise, keep in mind these tips:

- Wait for good timing. If the boss is rushed or in a bad mood, it is probably not a good time to bring it up.
- Schedule a meeting and prepare your talking points.
- Be confidant and firm, but not arrogant or entitled.

- Follow up in an email with the details of your conversation, what was agreed on, and the next steps.
- Be gracious and thank the boss.

Work with Your Physician

Depending on your physician, you may want to schedule an appointment to meet with them to explain your situation and fill out the paperwork, or at least have a conversation about it. My doctor has a patient advocate who I worked closely with. Inform them of your deadlines and follow up if needed.

Work Smarter, not Harder

Flares, or sudden, severe onsets of AI disease-related symptoms, present a unique challenge. Make judicious use of your sick and vacation time. If you sense a flare coming on, you may want to take a day or two off to manage it early rather than waiting until you're in a full-blown episode.

Document EVERYTHING

It's always a good idea to document everything. Even in the most perfect of work situations, you never know what tomorrow may bring. It's best to have the historical documentation to fall back on.

Track all of your absences. I used a spreadsheet to include the date, type of absence (annual leave, sick leave, FMLA, etc) and the reason (flare-up, doctors appointment, etc). I also kept track of my personal leave. While I'm not saying you should deny yourself of vacation time, if your leave balance is at a minimum, it is not prudent to be jet-setting off to Hawaii for a two week vacation. It's all about optics and you never know who is watching.

Find Your Support System at Work

Ask, "Who is my advocate?" You may have to ask several people or contact several offices, but find out who your advocate is. There were many individuals who I spoke with throughout my process who were "neutral parties." None were advocating on my behalf.

Find others in the same situation and ask them about their experiences. Ideally this would be at the same company, but it helps to have someone walk you through the process who is a few steps ahead of you.

Find Your Support System at Home

Ask your spouse, children, parents, friends, and/or neighbors for help and support. Do you remember the old adage of putting the oxygen mask on first? Your support system starts with YOU, so be sure to take care of yourself. Eat healthy, go for a walk, take a bath, do some yoga, go to church, meditate, get a massage. Whatever it takes, you have to take care of YOU first, even if that means asking those who love you for help so you have time for self-care.

Be Your Own Best Friend

I wanted to end on a strong note of self-care so I turned to Megan Buer, CECP, and founder of Harmony Restored, a company focused on helping individuals heal from the stress that is at the root of their physical and emotional pain. Megan shares:

"After years of struggling and trying to "fix" my autoimmune disease diagnosis, I found myself more stressed, exhausted, and anxious than I had ever been in my life. I spent every waking hour researching and trying to find the answers to my health questions. After much introspection, I realized I was looking outside of myself for answers. Basically, I was waiting for someone else to tell me what to do.

"A huge lesson I learned during my illness was that I had to show up for myself. I started looking at my symptoms as opportunities to step into my power, not to shrink and feel victimized. I had to dig deep and create space for my body and mind to thrive. Learning to truly love and take care of yourself is one of the greatest gifts that can come out of an autoimmune disease diagnosis.

"Denying your own power is a deep form of self-rejection and denial. Only when we are in a place of empowered self-care, can we thrive in service, charity, and love for others. Authentic self-care can take many forms: advocating for yourself at home and in the workplace, nourishing your body with healthy foods, creating joy, and taking time for rest and rejuvenation. It is only when we are standing in the flow of our own personal power that we can truly thrive."

RESOURCES

The following is a thorough, but not exhaustive list of resources you can tap into. If I were in your shoes, and you do need to reach out for help, my first stop would be to the Job Accommodation Network (askjan.org). I tried many different times to contact the FMLA and EEOC offices, and never got through to a human. Imagine going through what I went through. I was exhausted. My health was plummeting. My job was in jeopardy. We were worried about our finances and equally as worried about me ending up in the hospital. I tried to reach out to the agencies that are there to help me.

I spent a total of THREE hours on hold (different times and days) before I gave up. It was extremely frustrating. I called JAN and they picked up right away. The representatives were pleasant and helpful, and they even called me back just to check in.

CHAPTER 16
JOB ACCOMMODATION NETWORK

The Job Accommodation Network (JAN) is the leading source of free, expert, and confidential guidance on workplace accommodations and disability employment issues. Working toward practical solutions that benefit both employer and employee, JAN helps people with disabilities enhance their employability, and shows employers how to capitalize on the value and talent that people with disabilities add to the workplace.

For information on how to accommodate a specific individual with a disability, contact the Job Accommodation Network at:

- https://askjan.org/
- (800) 526-7234 (voice)
- (877) 781-9403 (TTY)

When I reached out to JAN to provide information specific to their resources for individuals with AI, this is what they offered:

JAN offers an extensive website populated with accommodation and ADA information that can empower individuals with autoimmune conditions to request accommodations at work.

The following JAN resources are useful for learning more about the process of requesting and negotiating reasonable accommodations:

- JAN's Employees' Practical Guide to Requesting and Negotiating Reasonable Accommodations Under the Americans with Disabilities Act (ADA) at http://AskJAN.org/EeGuide/
- JAN's How to Request an Accommodation Under the ADA at http://AskJAN.org/media/accommrequestltr.html

AskJAN.org makes it easy to find information about requesting and negotiating accommodations, the ADA, and accommodation solutions by disability or limitation. Of course, JAN consultants are available to provide individualized, free accommodation and ADA consultation over the phone, via email, or using live chat, but the Website is a great place to begin searching for useful resources. While the site does not offer a comprehensive list of accommodations by autoimmune conditions in general, it does offer a number of publications related to some specific autoimmune impairments.

For a general list of impairments, visit Accommodation Information by Disability: A to Z at https://askjan.org/media/atoz.htm. Examples of JAN accommodation resources related to autoimmune conditions include the following:

- Diabetes
- Fibromyalgia
- Gastrointestinal Disorders
- Graves' Disease
- Guillain-Barré Syndrome
- Lupus
- Lyme Disease
- Multiple Sclerosis
- Myasthenia Gravis
- Raynaud's Phenomenon
- Sarcoidosis
- Skin Disorders
- Thyroid Disorders.

CHAPTER 17
GOVERNMENT RESOURCES

Equal Employment Opportunity Commission

ADA Title I: Employment
Charges of employment discrimination on the basis of disability may be filed at any U.S. Equal Employment Opportunity Commission field office. Field offices are located in 50 cities throughout the U.S. and are listed in most telephone directories under "U.S. Government."

For the appropriate EEOC field office in your geographic area, contact:
- www.eeoc.gov
- https://www.eeoc.gov/contact/index.cfm
- http://www.eeoc.gov/facts/ada18.html
- http://www.eeoc.gov/facts/jobapplicant.html
- (800) 669-4000 (voice)
- (800) 669-6820 (TTY)
- info@eeoc.gov

ADA Title II: State and Local Government

Complaints of title II violations may be filed with the Department of Justice within 180 days of the date of discrimination. In certain situations, cases may be referred to a mediation program sponsored by the Department. The Department may bring a lawsuit where it has investigated a matter and has been unable to resolve violations.

Title II may also be enforced through private lawsuits in Federal court. It is not necessary to file a complaint with the Department of Justice (DOJ) or any other Federal agency, or to receive a "right-to-sue" letter, before going to court.

For more information, contact:
- www.ada.gov
- (800) 514-0301 (voice)
- (800) 514-0383 (TTY)

U.S. Department of Justice
Civil Rights Division
950 Pennsylvania Avenue, N.W.
Disability Rights Section - NYAV
Washington, D.C. 20530

Family Medical Leave Act

The U.S. Department of Labor's Wage and Hour Division (WHD) is responsible for administering and enforcing some of the nation's most important worker protection laws. WHD is committed to ensuring that workers in this country are paid properly and for all the hours they work, regardless of immigration status.

For more information contact:
- https://www.dol.gov/whd/fmla/
- http://dol.gov/whd/fmla/employeeguide.htm
- https://www.dol.gov/whd/contact_us.htm
- 1-866-4USWAGE (1-866-487-9243)
- TTY: 1-877-889-5627

CHAPTER 18
ADDITIONAL RESOURCES

<u>American Autoimmune Related Diseases Association, Inc</u>

The American Autoimmune Related Diseases Association is dedicated to the eradication of autoimmune diseases and the alleviation of suffering and the socioeconomic impact of autoimmunity through fostering and facilitating collaboration in the areas of education, public awareness, research, and patient services in an effective, ethical, and efficient manner.

For more information contact:
- https://www.aarda.org/
- https://www.aarda.org/contact/
- (586) 776-3900
- aarda@aarda.org

Invisible Disabilities Association

The Invisible Disabilities® Association is about believing. We believe you! The frequently invisible nature of illness and pain may lead to disbelief about that illness or pain by those surrounding the person who lives daily with invisible disabilities. This disbelief can lead to misunderstandings, rejection by friends, family and heath care providers. It may also lead to accusations of laziness or faking an illness. We are passionate about providing awareness that invisible illness, pain and disabilities are very real! Our mission is to encourage, educate and connect people and organizations touched by illness, pain and disability around the globe. Envision with us, a world where people living with illness, pain and disability will be Invisible No More®.

For more information contact:
- https://invisibledisabilities.org/
- https://invisibledisabilities.org/about/contact/

Patient Advocate Foundation

Patient Advocate Foundation's Patient Services provides patients with arbitration, mediation and negotiation to settle issues with access to care, medical debt, and job retention related to their illness.

For more information contact:
- http://www.patientadvocate.org/
- http://www.patientadvocate.org/index.php?p=758
- (800) 532-5274

FINAL THOUGHTS

Our employment is important to us – financially, socially, and emotionally. But at the end of the day, it's just a job. It's not faith. It's not family. It's not health.

When you have AI or any kind of chronic illness, there is only so much of you to give out. As you are figuring out this process, always remember to take care of yourself. There is only one you. And you need to step up and take care of yourself before you can take care of anyone else. If you take away only one concept from this book, let it be that. Because you deserve it.

I hope this book brings you closer to finding that balance in your life to be able to take care of yourself. I hope this book gives you the resources you need to further educate yourself. I hope this book lays out a real picture of what you are facing. I hope this book gives you a voice. I hope this book helps you to understand that you are not alone. And I hope this book gives you hope.

Blessings to you, my friend, as you continue your journey.

I love feedback, so please leave a review on Amazon, or drop me a note.

You can reach me at holly@pinkfortitude.com or hit me up on social media @PinkFortitude

Thank you for letting me be a part of your quest for a healthier you.

Holly Bertone, CHNP, PMP

THANK YOU for your purchase! As a small gesture of our extreme gratitude, please accept your free eBook (and other goodies!) to launch you into the life of good health and fortitude!
Download your FREE book here:
https://pinkfortitude.com/thank/

THRIVE ONLINE!

Visit http://pinkfortitude.com/**ThriveAI** for all of your online resources associated with this book.

BIBLIOGRAPHY AND SOURCES

Interviews:

Buer, Megan, CECP, Founder of Harmony Restored:
https://go.harmony-restored.com/free-giftl9l0a6qo

DeFreitas, Tracie, MS, CLMS, Lead Consultant, ADA
Specialist at the Job Accommodation Network:
https://askjan.org/

Websites:

American Autoimmune Related Disease Association:
https://www.aarda.org/
Americans with Disabilities Act:
- https://www.ada.gov/
- https://www.ada.gov/enforce_current.htm
- https://www.eeoc.gov/laws/statutes/adaaa.cfm
- https://www.ada.gov/cguide.htm

United States Department of Justice:
https://www.justice.gov/crt/disability-rights-section

United States Department of Labor:
- https://www.dol.gov/odep/pubs/fact/ydw.htm
- https://www.dol.gov/whd/fmla/

Equal Employment Opportunity Commission:
- https://www.eeoc.gov/eeoc/
- http://www.eeoc.gov/facts/ada18.html
- http://www.eeoc.gov/facts/jobapplicant.html
- https://www.eeoc.gov/facts/performance-conduct.html
- https://www.eeoc.gov/laws/types/disability.cfm
- https://www.eeoc.gov/laws/statutes/adaaa.cfm
- https://www.eeoc.gov/policy/docs/accommodation.html

Job Accommodation Network:
- https://askjan.org/
- https://askjan.org/topics/discl.htm

Legal Works Cited:

Smith, Levenski R. "FindLaw's United States Eighth Circuit Case and Opinions." *Findlaw*. N.p., n.d. Web. 20 July 2017.

Sweeney, Dennis J. "FindLaw's Court of Appeals of Washington Case and Opinions." *Findlaw*. N.p., n.d. Web. 22 July 2017.

ABOUT THE AUTHOR

Holly Bertone, CNHP, PMP, is a #1 Amazon.com bestselling author and health entrepreneur. She is the President and CEO of Pink Fortitude, LLC and runs the health and wellness website pinkfortitude.com. Holly is a breast cancer and Hashimoto's survivor and turned these two significant health challenges into a passion to help others. She inspires others with her quick wit, brutal honesty, and simple ways to be healthy in real life.

Holly is a Certified Natural Health Professional and is enrolled in a Naturopathic Doctorate program. She holds a Masters Degree from Johns Hopkins University, a Bachelor's Degree from Elizabethtown College, and is a Project Management Professional (PMP).

Holly is passionate about reaching out to cancer and autoimmune survivors, and also volunteers for organizations supporting our military veterans. In her free time, she loves to garden, and hit flea markets and yard sales. Holly is married to a retired Green Beret, is a stepmother, and lives in Alexandria, VA.

Other Books by Holly Bertone

Coconut Head's Survival Guide: My Journey from Diagnosis to "I Do."
Drops of Fortitude: Find Your Inner Strength During Cancer Treatment
My Mommy Has Cancer
How to Make the Transition to a Healthy Lifestyle

22958741R00054